P9-BJV-928

GETTING TO KNOW THE WORLD'S GREATEST
INVENTORS **&** SCIENTISTS

H E N R Y
FORD

Big Wheel in the Auto Industry

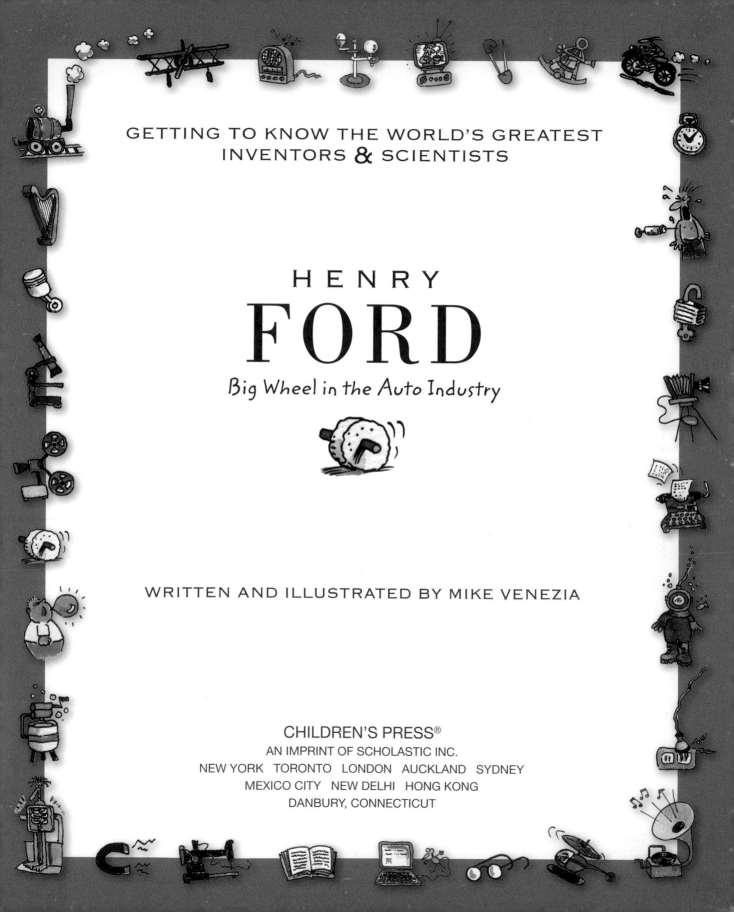

WRITTEN AND ILLUSTRATED BY MIKE VENEZIA

CHILDREN'S PRESS®
AN IMPRINT OF SCHOLASTIC INC.
NEW YORK TORONTO LONDON AUCKLAND SYDNEY
MEXICO CITY NEW DELHI HONG KONG
DANBURY, CONNECTICUT

Reading Consultant: Nanci R. Vargus, Ed.D., Assistant Professor, School of Education, University of Indianapolis

Content Consultant: Joyce Bedi, Senior Historian, Lemelson Center for the Study of Invention and Innovation, National Museum of American History, Smithsonian Institution

Photographs © 2009: Corbis Images: 15, 20 (Bettmann), 25 (PoodlesRock), 30 top (Underwood & Underwood); Everett Collection, Inc.: 26 (Keystone/Eyedea), 22 top right; Getty Images: 23 (AFP), 17, 24 (Hulton Archive), 30 bottom (Time & Life Pictures); North Wind Picture Archives: 10; Photo Researchers, NY/Kenneth Murray: 27 top, 27 bottom; Superstock, Inc./Roy King: 28; The Granger Collection, New York: 3, 22 bottom; From the Collections of The Henry Ford: 6 bottom, 6 top, 12, 13, 14, 19, 31; The Image Works: 21 (Mary Evans Picture Library), 22 top left (SSPL).

Colorist for illustrations: Andrew Day

Library of Congress Cataloging-in-Publication Data

Venezia, Mike.
  Henry Ford : big wheel in the auto industry / written and illustrated by Mike Venezia.
      p. cm. — (Getting to know the world's greatest inventors and scientists)
  Includes index.
  ISBN-13: 978-0-531-23726-7 (lib. bdg.)   978-0-531-21335-3 (pbk.)
  ISBN-10: 0-531-23726-5 (lib. bdg.)   0-531-21335-8 (pbk.)
  1. Ford, Henry, 1863-1947—Juvenile literature. 2. Automobile engineers—United States—Biography—Juvenile literature. 3. Industrialists—United States—Biography—Juvenile literature. 4. Automobile industry and trade—United States—Biography—Juvenile literature. I. Title.
  TL140.F6V45 2009
  338.7'6292092—dc22
  [B]
                          2008027651

No part of this publication may be reproduced in whole or in part, or stored in a retrieval system, or transmitted in any form or by any means, electronic, mechanical, photocopying, recording, or otherwise, without written permission of the publisher. For information regarding permission, write to Scholastic Inc., 557 Broadway, New York, NY 10012.

© 2009 by Mike Venezia.

All rights reserved. Published in 2009 by Children's Press, an imprint of Scholastic Inc. Published simultaneously in Canada. Printed in the United States of America.

SCHOLASTIC, CHILDREN'S PRESS, and associated logos are trademarks and/or registered trademarks of Scholastic Inc.

1 2 3 4 5 6 7 8 9 10 R 18 17 16 15 14 13 12 11 10 09

Henry Ford's Model T, produced from 1908 to 1927, has been called the car that "put America on wheels." Here Ford is shown with a 1920 Model T.

Henry Ford was born on July 30, 1863, on his parents' farm in Greenfield Township, Michigan. Henry was the first person to make dependable automobiles that were affordable enough for just about any American family to own. He forever changed transportation and the way **manufacturing** is done.

Today it's almost impossible to imagine a world without cars. Before Henry Ford was born, most moving vehicles were powered by horses

or mules. When Henry started
manufacturing millions of cars,
he pretty much put most horses
out of business.

Henry Ford as a young boy

While Henry was growing up on his family's farm, some neighbors said he was the laziest boy they had ever seen. Sometimes Henry would leave his chores to get a drink of water and then never come back. Henry hated hard farm work and would do anything to avoid it.

An 1876 illustration of the Ford family farm in Michigan

Henry would much rather spend time in his father's work shed, thinking up ways to use machines to make farm work easier. He loved to tinker with anything mechanical. Unlike other kids, Henry's favorite toys were tools, nuts and bolts, and machine parts!

Henry Ford said that the biggest event of his life happened when he was twelve years old. While traveling to the nearby city of Detroit, Henry and his father saw a huge, chugging, clanking, steam-driven engine coming down the road toward them. It was the first **self-propelled** vehicle Henry had ever seen.

Henry couldn't believe his eyes! He jumped out of his father's wagon and began asking the engineer, Fred Reden, a thousand questions about how the engine worked. Later that year, Mr. Reden let Henry drive the steam machine.

This illustration shows an American farmer using a steam-powered plow in the 1890s.

In the late 1800s, **portable steam engines** were hooked up to operate sawmills, **threshing machines**, and other equipment. Henry loved the idea of a machine that could make farm work easier. He was even more fascinated by the idea of a machine that could travel down the road on its own power.

The day he saw the self-propelled steam engine, Henry decided he would become a **machinist** — someone who builds and repairs machines. Henry began practicing by building small steam engines. He also worked on his mechanical skills by fixing his neighbors' pocket watches. He even made his own tiny tools to repair watches.

In his late teens, Henry Ford worked as an apprentice machinist at the Detroit Dry Dock Company. This photograph shows Ford (top row, sixth from right) with other company workers in 1880.

Henry was always itching to get away from the farm. When he was sixteen, he left home and traveled to Detroit. Detroit was a busy industrial city. Henry **apprenticed** at different **machine shops** there to learn everything he could about mechanics.

After about three years, Henry returned to the farm. It was a busy time for him. His father gave him forty acres of land, and Henry set up a sawmill there. Henry also got a job running and repairing the same type of moveable steam engine that had inspired him as a boy. Henry began thinking more seriously about building a **horseless carriage**.

During this time, Henry met his future wife. Her name was Clara Bryant. Clara and Henry met at a local town dance. After dating for a while, the couple got married, on April 11, 1888.

Henry's wife, Clara Bryant Ford

As an engineer with the Edison Illuminating Company, Ford (third from the left, on the ground) worked on steam engines that helped provide electric power.

Clara was the perfect wife for Henry. She understood her husband's dream to build a horseless carriage someday. Clara agreed to leave their cozy farmhouse and move to Detroit. Henry knew he could learn more about engines there, and it was easier to have machine parts made in Detroit.

Henry got a job right away at the Edison Illuminating Company, which built electric power stations. Henry worked there as an **engineer** and machinist. In his spare time, he read everything he could find about building engines. At home, Henry began working on a gasoline engine that would someday power his horseless carriage.

Henry Ford developed his first horseless carriage in a shed behind his home in Detroit. Today, a replica of this workshop (above) is on display at Greenfield Village in Dearborn, Michigan.

Some people think Henry Ford invented the gasoline engine, but he didn't. The gasoline engine, or **internal combustion engine**, was invented just before Henry was born. That kind of engine wasn't used very often, though. At that time, gasoline engines weren't very powerful or dependable. But Henry still thought they could be better than steam engines. Gasoline engines were much smaller and more portable. A steam-powered vehicle needed to carry around big loads of wood or coal to fuel a boiler in order to make steam. Henry believed he could design a better gasoline engine that would be perfect for his horseless carriage.

Henry Ford didn't invent the automobile, either. A few carmakers had been around for years, but their cars were too expensive for most Americans to own. Also, these early cars were hard to handle

The first four-wheeled, gas-powered car (above) was built by Wilhelm Maybach and Gottlieb Daimler in 1886. Only very wealthy people could afford the earliest cars.

and broke down a lot. There were also a small number of cars built for racing, which was just starting to become a popular sport. Henry's goal was to make a car that was reliable and was cheap enough for anyone to own.

In November of 1893, Clara and Henry's only child, Edsel, was born. He was named after a boyhood friend of Henry's, Edsel Ruddiman. About a month later, on Christmas Eve, another exciting event happened. Henry brought his first gasoline engine into the kitchen so he could test it out.

Ford started up his first gasoline-powered engine (above) on his kitchen table in 1893. A later version of that engine powered his first automobile in 1896.

Henry needed electricity from the kitchen light socket to spark the engine's fuel. Clara helped by carefully dripping gasoline into the engine. Suddenly, it started up. The engine worked great! A few days later, Henry started building a bigger engine that would be powerful enough to run a vehicle. Then, with the help of some mechanic friends, Henry built a frame with bicycle wheels, a seat, and steering stick called a **tiller**. In 1896, Henry took his first horseless carriage for a test ride down the streets of Detroit.

Henry Ford sits in his pride and joy, the 1896 Quadricycle.

Henry called his first car a **quadricycle**. When the mayor of Detroit saw the quadricycle, he was so impressed that he offered to raise money to start up an automobile company with Henry. It was called the Detroit Automobile Company. It didn't last very long, though. Neither did Henry's next company, the Henry Ford Company.

One problem was that not enough people knew about Henry's cars. Henry decided to fix that problem right away. He began to build race cars. Henry knew that people were crazy about car races. When Henry entered his first race, he surprised everyone by finishing in first place! Suddenly there were lots of newspaper stories about Henry Ford and his hot new racer.

Ford sits behind the wheel of one of his racing cars (at left) during a race in 1903.

A 1903 Ford Model A

A 1906 Ford Model N

Winning races really helped Henry Ford's cars get attention. He started a third company, the Ford Motor Company, and it became a huge success! Henry hired lots of workers and began making a car called the Model A. People loved this simple, well-made car. Soon Henry and his chief designer, Childe Wills, began developing other car models.

A 1919 Ford Model T

Henry and his son Edsel in a Model F in 1905

Henry named his first cars after letters of the alphabet. There were the models A, B, C, F, N, R, S, K, and one of the most popular cars ever made, the Model T. Now Henry's biggest problem was how to make enough cars for the thousands of people who wanted one. This challenge helped Henry Ford come up with his most important idea.

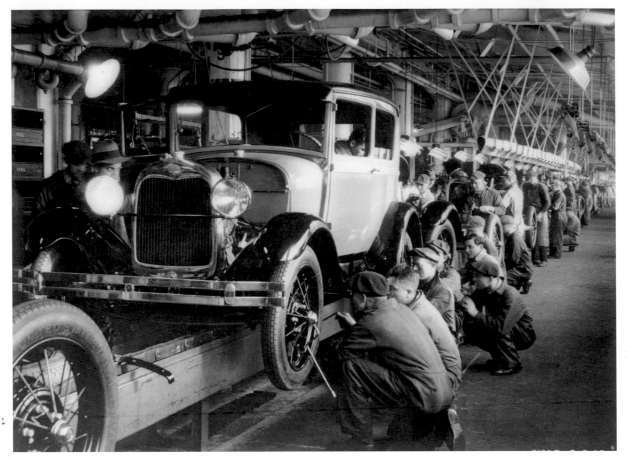

Workers on a Ford assembly line in 1927

Henry Ford began using **assembly lines** to manufacture his cars. Henry didn't invent the assembly line, but he brought this process to carmaking. Up until that time, a group of workers would collect all the parts needed to build a car. Together they'd build an entire car before moving on to building the next car. Sometimes it took a long time to build one car because they had to wait for a certain part to arrive.

In an assembly line, however, each worker was assigned one small part of the job, such as putting on a wheel or tightening a bolt. Each worker would perform his task over and over as car after car rolled slowly by on a **conveyer line**. Finally, at the end of the assembly line, a finished car would be ready to ship out. Assembly lines made it possible to triple the number of cars that could be made in a day. Making more cars more quickly allowed Henry to drop the price of his cars, too.

THE FORD MOTOR PLANT.
AND 1,000 CARS, A SINGLE DAYS OUTPUT.

As this postcard boasts, 1,000 Model Ts were produced each day at the Ford Motor Plant in 1916.

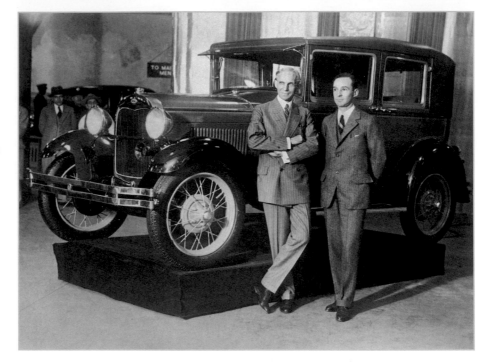

When he grew up, Edsel Ford (right) helped his father (left) run the Ford Motor Company. Here they are shown in 1928, with the first Model A.

Things were going great for Henry. By 1927, 15 million Model T Fords had been manufactured. Edsel was now helping his father run the business. Edsel thought it was time to make a new, more modern car. Henry agreed, and together they came up with another winner, the new Model A Ford.

By this time, Henry had built a factory on the Rouge River in Dearborn, Michigan. To handle all the Model A orders, Henry expanded this plant. Soon it manufactured not just cars, but also steel and other raw materials. It even had its own electric power plant.

The River Rouge plant was so awesome that famous artists of the time often painted pictures of it.

World-famous Mexican artist Diego Rivera showed the Ford Motor Company's River Rouge plant in his mural *Detroit Industry*. At right and below are details from this mural, which can be seen at the Detroit Institute of the Arts.

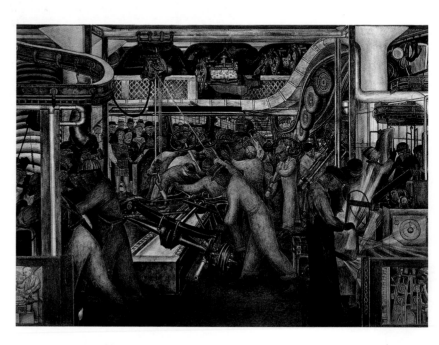

By the 1930s, Ford was facing competition from other car manufacturers, including Chevrolet. This is a 1935 Chevrolet.

Henry Ford's company kept growing and growing. His dream had become a reality. Things weren't always perfect, though. By 1930, some competitors had also built large auto companies. Some cool-looking cars, like Chevrolets, began to take business away from Ford.

Also, assembly lines had made production faster, but many workers became bored doing the same old thing all day long. Some workers were so unhappy that they quit after a short time.

Henry tried to improve things by paying higher salaries and shortening the workday. But the situation never really got much better. Some critics blamed Henry for air pollution and annoying traffic jams, too.

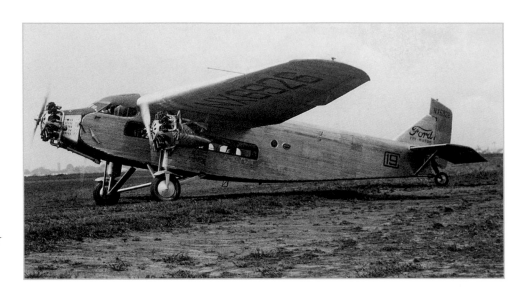

A 1930s
Ford tri-motor
airplane

Henry Ford eventually branched out into making other kinds of vehicles. He built passenger planes, tractors, and trucks. During World War I and World War II, Ford supplied the U.S. military with ambulances, cars, trucks, airplane engines, bomber planes, and tanks. Today, the Ford Motor Company is still one of the top carmakers in the world.

A 1940s Ford tractor with a
hole-digging attachment

Near the end of his life, Henry spent more and more time away from his company. He enjoyed adding to his collections of machinery and other historic objects at the Henry Ford Museum and Greenfield Village in Dearborn, Michigan. Greenfield Village is an outdoor museum where visitors can still learn about American life as Henry Ford remembered it from his earliest days. In 1947, Henry Ford died peacefully in his home at the age of 83.

Henry Ford (at right) and his son Edsel sit and relax by a fireplace at Greenfield Village in 1941.

Glossary

apprentice (uh-PREN-tiss) To learn a trade or craft by working with a skilled person

assembly line (uh-SEM-blee LINE) A manufacturing method in which each worker or machine completes only a small part of the whole process

conveyor line (kuhn-VAY-ur LINE) A moving belt or chain that carries objects from one place to another in a factory

engineer (en-juh-NIHR) A person who designs and builds engines

horseless carriage (HORSS-less KA-rij) An early name for the automobile

internal combustion engine (in-TUR-nuhl kuhm-BUSS-chuhn EN-juhn) An engine that is powered by the burning of gasoline or other fuel inside the engine

machine shop (muh-SHEEN SHOP) A workshop where machine parts are made or repaired

machinist (muh-SHEE-nist) A person who makes or repairs machinery

manufacturing (man-yoo-FACK-chur-ing) The making of things in large quantities, often with the use of machinery

portable steam engine (POR-tuh-buhl STEEM EN-juhn) An easily moved engine that uses steam to create power; the steam is created by burning coal or wood to heat water in a tank

quadricycle (KWAD-ruh-sye-kuhl) Henry Ford's first internal-combustion-engine car

self-propelled (SELF pruh-PELD) Able to move forward by its own power

threshing machine (THRESH-ing muh-SHEEN) A machine that separates grain from stalks and husks

tiller (TIL-uhr) A steering stick used in boats and in early automobiles

Index